Advance Praise for

A BEAVER TALE

"In his new children's book titled *A Beaver Tale: The Castors of Conners Creek*, Gerald Wykes has freshly told the amazing story of the return of beavers to the Detroit River. Through compelling narrative and lively illustrations, *A Beaver Tale* will teach children about the cleanup and recovery of the Detroit River and do it in a fashion where they may even realize that if the Detroit River is cleaner for beaver, it is cleaner for each of us because we live in the same ecosystem."

—John Hartig, refuge manager of the
Detroit River International Wildlife Refuge

"*A Beaver Tale* is an accurate account of the surprising reappearance of beavers in Detroit after 150 years. Gerry Wykes's artistic talent brings the beavers to life with engaging illustrations, and the beaver facts will help us all to become beaver experts. As Gerry says at the end of the book, 'Let's hear it for the beavers!'"

—Roberta Urbani, retired DTE Energy environmental planner
and 2013 *Detroit Free Press* Michigan Green Leader

A BEAVER TALE

Great Lakes Books

Editor

Charles K. Hyde
Wayne State University

Advisory Editors

Jeffrey Abt
Wayne State University

Fredric C. Bohm
Michigan State University

Sandra Sageser Clark
Michigan Historical Center

Brian Leigh Dunnigan
Clements Library

De Witt Dykes
Oakland University

Joe Grimm
Michigan State University

Richard H. Harms
Calvin College

Laurie Harris
Pleasant Ridge, Michigan

Thomas Klug
Marygrove College

Susan Higman Larsen
Detroit Institute of Arts

Philip P. Mason
Prescott, Arizona and Eagle Harbor, Michigan

Dennis Moore
Consulate General of Canada

Erik C. Nordberg
Michigan Humanities Council

Deborah Smith Pollard
University of Michigan–Dearborn

Michael O. Smith
Wayne State University

Joseph M. Turrini
Wayne State University

Arthur M. Woodford
Harsens Island, Michigan

A complete listing of the books in this series can be found online at wsupress.wayne.edu

A BEAVER TALE
THE CASTORS OF CONNERS CREEK

Written and Illustrated by Gerald Wykes

Wayne State University Press | Detroit

20 19 18 17 16   5 4 3 2 1

Library of Congress Control Number: 2015959339

ISBN 978-0-8143-4181-0 (cloth)
ISBN 978-0-8143-4182-7 (ebook)

Designed and typeset by Bryce Schimanski
Composed in Adobe Caslon Pro

A BEAVER TALE

Every native tribe had a different name for the beaver. The Anishnaabe word was *amik*. Wyandots used the term *tsooh-tah-ih*—meaning "shiny ones." French fur traders called them *castors*, which was their word for beaver. The French name is still widely used today as an alternate name for beaver and is even part of their scientific name— *Castor canadensis*.

In 2008, the members of Detroit's Edison Boat Club had a mystery on their hands. Someone, or something, was cutting down their trees, creating open gaps where tall cottonwoods once stood. It looked like the work of a beaver, but that seemed impossible. After all, this was the east side of Detroit. There hadn't been a beaver here in 150 years! They thought the suspect surely must be someone using a chainsaw in a way that made it look like a beaver chewing. A Bigfoot would have been a more believable suspect.

Beavers were once one of the most important animals in Michigan, North America, and even the world. In the 1700s, their pelts were used as a form of money and as material for expensive hats. In fact, Detroit was built over 300 years ago largely to handle the business of the beaver trade. At that time, beavers were better known by their French name of *castors*. The Detroit River castors soon disappeared as trapping increased, decimating their population, and the town grew bigger and bigger. Even after the beaver trade ended in the 1800s, the beavers could not return to their old home. Factories had sprung up where forests once grew, and the river water was now polluted from the city's waste.

Growth exploded after the invention of the automobile in the early 1900s. Energy plants were constructed to provide electricity for the many new industries and people moving to Detroit. The giant Conners Creek Power Plant was built in 1914 on a piece of marshy ground just east of the city. The waters of the Detroit River cooled the massive generators and offered a highway for Great Lakes ships delivering mountains of coal used to fire the generators. Three centuries since its founding, the city, once built thanks to the beaver, was no longer a beaver-friendly place.

The Edison Boat Club sits on the mighty Detroit River next to the towering chimneys and buildings of the Conners Creek Power Plant. Many of its members work, or once worked, for the DTE Energy Company. Soon after the tree mystery began, a few club members glimpsed something that looked like a beaver swimming in the water around their boats, but they couldn't be sure. Workers at Conners Creek also noticed some missing trees and strange critters swimming near the plant so they asked the DTE "Green Team" to look into it.

The Green Team is a group of company employees and volunteers who work on special wildlife habitat projects in the Detroit area. Green Team member Jason Cousino got the job of solving the mystery of who, or what, the tree thief was. Jason had encountered coyotes, ospreys, and angry tree swallows over the years, but never beavers. Expecting that someone was playing a trick, he began his investigation in early November. He was astonished to see cleanly cut wood and clear tooth marks on the tree trunks. This was not the work of a person or a Bigfoot—it was definitely the work of a big-toothed beaver.

Jason was excited. He quickly got in touch with local wildlife officials, who doubted his story. But when he sent them a clear photo of the chewed trees with the tall towers of Detroit's well-known Renaissance Center in the background, they agreed that a real live beaver had, indeed, returned to the city of Detroit.

Next, Jason set out to "capture" the animal on video. He pointed a night vision trail camera at one of the partly chewed trees. If the beaver returned to finish the job, the camera would automatically catch him in the act. The next morning, Jason found what he was looking for on the camera's tiny memory card. There, in a short black-and-white video, was the unmistakable image of a large flat-tailed beaver hauling away one of the branches. With the twinkling lights of the river and city behind it, an unlikely movie star was born at 5:29 am on November 11, 2008.

Now everyone wanted to know if the beaver was just passing through or was planning on sticking around. Beavers often wander great distances, but don't normally cut down trees unless they are building a home. A beaver visiting Detroit was interesting enough, but a beaver returning to live in Detroit was real news! Jason, continuing his work as a wildlife detective, eventually found a newly made lodge (beaver home) along the banks of the old intake canal at Conners Creek, only a quarter-mile from where his "movie star" first made his video appearance. This beaver was settling in to be one of east-side Detroit's newest homeowners.

Jason and the Green Team officials kept their news quiet for the rest of the fall and early winter. They were worried that someone might try to disturb the animal and drive it away. As it turned out, the lodge was quite safe from unwanted human visitors, being located smack in the middle of the well-fenced property of the Conners Creek Power Plant and the boat club. There was even a security guard posted at the main gate. It was probably the best-protected beaver lodge in the world!

The following February, a *Detroit Free Press* reporter wrote a big story about the beaver's return, which quickly spread to print and internet media across the country. The face of Detroit's castor even made its way around the globe to Chinese newspapers.

One morning, Regis Philbin, co-host of the popular *Live with Regis and Kelly* television show, mentioned the Conners Creek story, loudly announcing, "Ladies and gentlemen, let's hear it for the beavers!" The studio audience cheered as did millions of viewers across the country. People seemed happy to hear some good news coming from a place that had seen a lot of bad news in the recent past.

Detroit, the beaver's new home, was trying to come back from hard times. The Detroit River had been heavily polluted, companies were going out of business, workers could not find work, and whole neighborhoods were abandoned. Instead of growing, the city population had shrunk back to where it was in 1914—the year the Conners Creek Power Plant was built!

Many people were busy working to clean up the river and make the city a better place. For them, this animal became a symbol of hope. If a beaver could rebuild, so could they! A Canadian reporter remarked that this busy beaver was a reminder that "with hard work, comebacks are possible."

The hard work that cleared the way for the beaver to come back to Detroit had been years in the making. Tough new environmental laws helped clear up the oil, chemical, and sewage pollution that had once poisoned the Detroit River water. In 1999, the Conners Creek Power Plant switched from burning dirty coal to burning cleaner natural gas. That meant that giant piles of coal disappeared, a huge section of the old plant was torn down, and the open grounds were allowed to grow over with grass and trees.

As the river gradually became cleaner and cleaner, several other long-absent native water animals, such as lake sturgeon, whitefish, and bald eagles, began returning to the area. The cleaner, healthier Detroit River was once again an animal-friendly (and beaver-friendly) place.

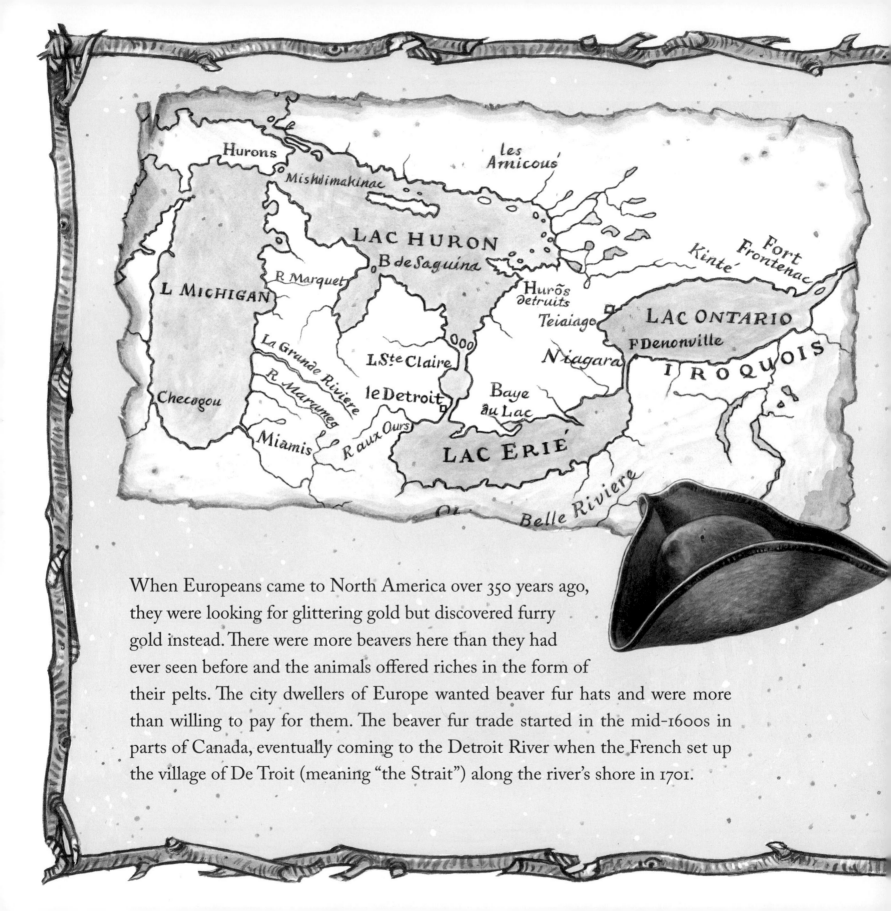

When Europeans came to North America over 350 years ago, they were looking for glittering gold but discovered furry gold instead. There were more beavers here than they had ever seen before and the animals offered riches in the form of their pelts. The city dwellers of Europe wanted beaver fur hats and were more than willing to pay for them. The beaver fur trade started in the mid-1600s in parts of Canada, eventually coming to the Detroit River when the French set up the village of De Troit (meaning "the Strait") along the river's shore in 1701.

Most of the trapping in the Great Lakes area was done by native tribes such as the Ottawa, Chippewa, and Pottawatomi, among others. They caught the beavers in the winter using steel traps and stretched their furs on willow hoops. They then traded the furs with French and English traders for food and other needed items.

Beaver was used as money in the barter days of Old Detroit. Goods such as food, silver trinkets, and wool blankets were given a price in beaver skins (called "made beaver") instead of a cash money price. A striped wool blanket, for instance, might cost two beavers, a silver cross one beaver, and a birch bark canoe could cost twelve pelts. Other kinds of animal pelts were also given a "beaver pelt value" using the barter system. Otter and Lynx pelts equaled two beaver pelts in value and it took around ten muskrats to equal one beaver.

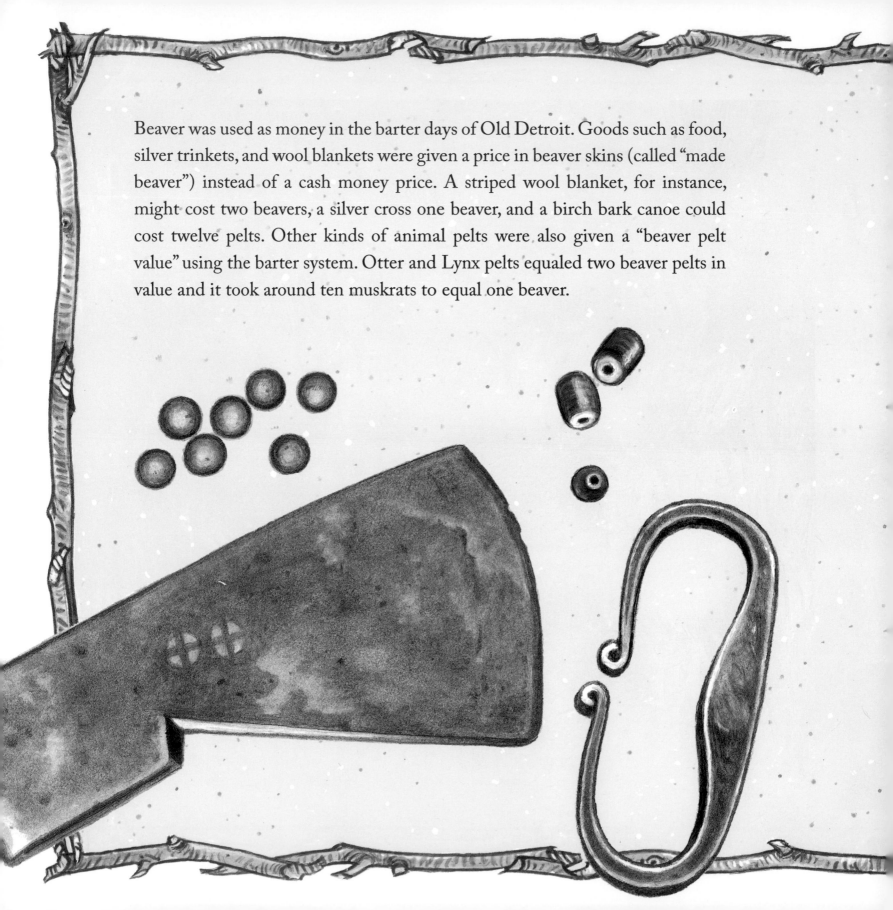

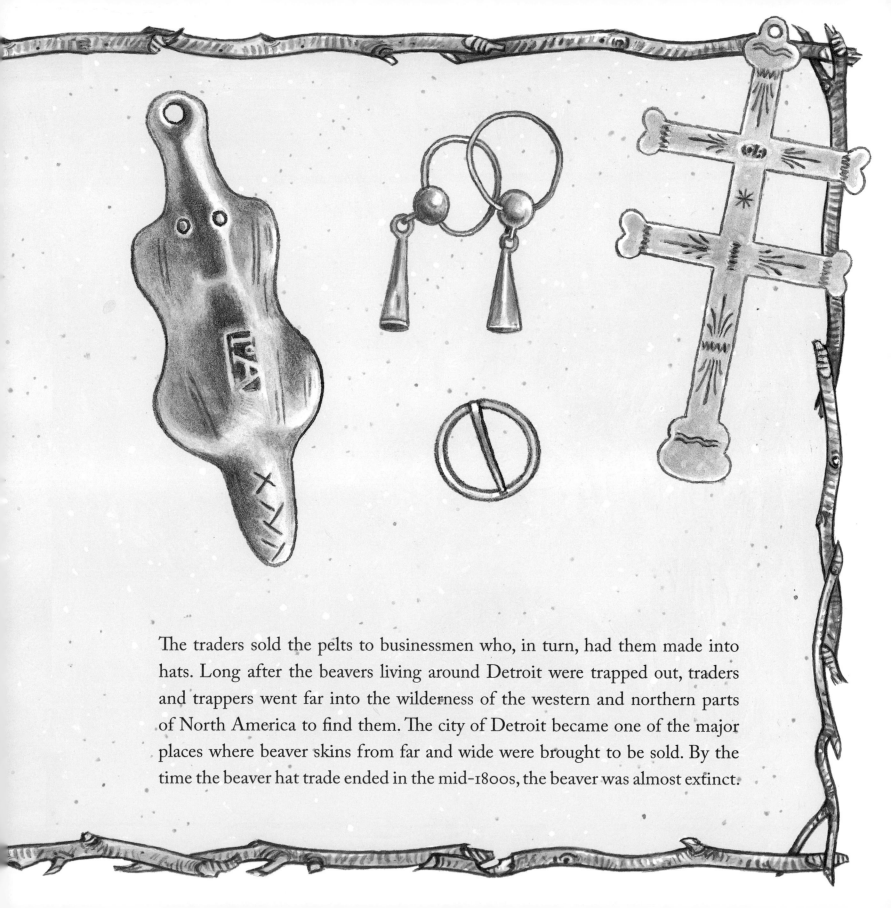

The traders sold the pelts to businessmen who, in turn, had them made into hats. Long after the beavers living around Detroit were trapped out, traders and trappers went far into the wilderness of the western and northern parts of North America to find them. The city of Detroit became one of the major places where beaver skins from far and wide were brought to be sold. By the time the beaver hat trade ended in the mid-1800s, the beaver was almost extinct.

All this history meant nothing to the curious creature that swam into the Conners Creek canal on that evening in 2008. All that mattered was that he found everything he needed to live. There were many cottonwood and willow trees, lots of clean water, and plenty of space to grow.

In the mind of a beaver, this was a perfect place to stay and raise a family. He couldn't have known that his arrival would cause such excitement among the humans living there. For that lone beaver, the future was all that mattered.

"Busy as a beaver" is a well-known saying. Beavers, like people, are always working to change the world around them. Sometimes, they act like engineers, building dams or digging canals. Human engineers did most of that kind of work at Conners Creek long ago, so this new beaver could focus all of his attention on improving his lodge and preparing it for starting a family.

With powerful jaws, he cut and trimmed trees like a skilled lumberman, dragging the branches through the water to the lodge roof. Clumps of mud, water plants, and rocks scraped from the canal bottom were packed into the spaces between the piled sticks. The beaver carried this material with his front paws, walking upright on his hind legs, as he put it into place.

The lodge grew to be about twenty feet around and six feet high. It was a little different from other beaver dwellings, however. This was the home of a city beaver after all. Scrap pieces of lumber, boat straps, a fishing pole, and even an old rake made up parts of the lodge. Perhaps its most unusual feature was the paneled ceiling. The lodge had been built around the end of an old "skimmer boom" lying on the shore. Similar to a seventy-foot fence held between two large floating telephone poles, the skimmer boom once kept leaves, sticks, and oil spills from floating down the canal and into the power plant's generators. The beaver dug two underwater doorway tunnels and an inner room, allowing the boards of the boom to form a slanted ceiling over half of the inside living area. The rest of the lodge had a natural stick-and-mud ceiling, a bark-covered floor, and two chimney holes poking through to the surface. The interior room would be just big enough to fit several human children, but only if they crouched down or laid flat on their stomachs.

Amazingly, it didn't take long before a second beaver, a female, arrived to inspect the new fancy homestead. She, apparently, liked what she saw and decided to stay. In the spring of 2009, the celebrity castor and his new mate became the proud parents of two "kits"—which is what baby beavers are called. The Green Team's trail cameras caught glimpses of the two little kits nibbling on leaves and walking around on their hind feet just like miniature adult beavers. Detroit's newest homeowners had become its newest family as well.

Life for the small beaver colony settled into a normal pattern. They worked, ate, played in the canal by night, and rested inside the lodge by day. Members of the Edison Boat Club, who rested by night and played by day, saw them only in the dim light of dawn or dusk. With the distant city sounds of overhead jets, sirens, and barking dogs in the background, the adult castors spent most of their long evening hours gathering fresh twigs for the coming winter. The twigs were pushed into the bottom mud near the lodge to create a mini-forest of food just outside their front door. When thick winter ice sealed over the surface of the canal all the way out to the Detroit River, these stick snacks kept the beaver family fat and happy through the winter.

Soon after the lodge was built, a family of muskrats moved into the lodge. The muskrats, tiny cousins of the beaver, created an apartment off to the side and raised several large families of fuzzy young each year. At times, the dark interior of the lodge must have been a hectic place as muskrat kits frolicked amongst the much larger beavers. Fortunately, the two families shared their space well and also shared some common enemies. Even along the banks of the urban canals of Detroit, mink, red fox, and coyote can be found looking for prey. Both animals also risked exposure to boats and their whirling propellers when swimming in the Detroit River.

The colony at Conners Creek will stay around as long as there is the right kind of tree bark to eat. While any tree will do for building, beavers can't survive without cottonwood or willow bark as food. The beavers cut down most of the nearby trees within the first few years, causing them to have to swim farther and farther away to find new ones. Some are well over a half mile away, which means more risky trips into the big waters of the Detroit River.

Even wilderness beaver colonies have to move every five to eight years as their food supply eventually runs out. New beavers then return years later after the trees have had a chance to grow back.

The city beavers called on their tree-farming skills to help make their supplies last as long as possible. Old tree stumps send out fast growing shoots within months of being cut, but those sprouts will not be big enough to provide bark until they are at least a year old. The castor "farmers" know to look elsewhere before returning to harvest these shoots the following year. This allows one tree to provide food for the beavers long after it was first cut down.

Due to hard work and careful planning, the Conners Creek beavers have lived several years now in their city neighborhood. They have raised multiple sets of kits over that time. Sometimes father, mother, last year's kits, and a new set of baby kits were all living in the colony at one time. Young beavers, however, get the urge to explore when they become "teenagers" at eighteen months. They are eager to try out their engineering, building, and tree-farming skills. So, when they came of age, just like their parents did years before, the Conners Creek kits entered the Detroit River and set off on their own. That is the beaver way.

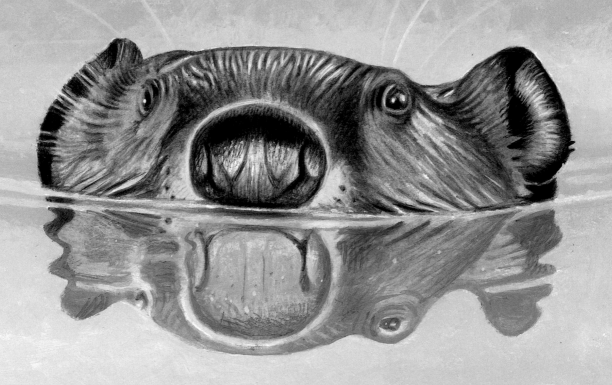

By 2013, new beavers began appearing on the shores of Detroit River islands and further downriver at DTE's River Rouge Power Plant. These beaver explorers are proving that this success story will continue to be told. Whatever the future brings, the castors of Conners Creek, who once captured the attention of the world, will always be remembered as the pioneers who helped bring the beaver back home to Detroit.

Let's hear it for the beavers!

More Facts about Beavers

A Beaver-built Place

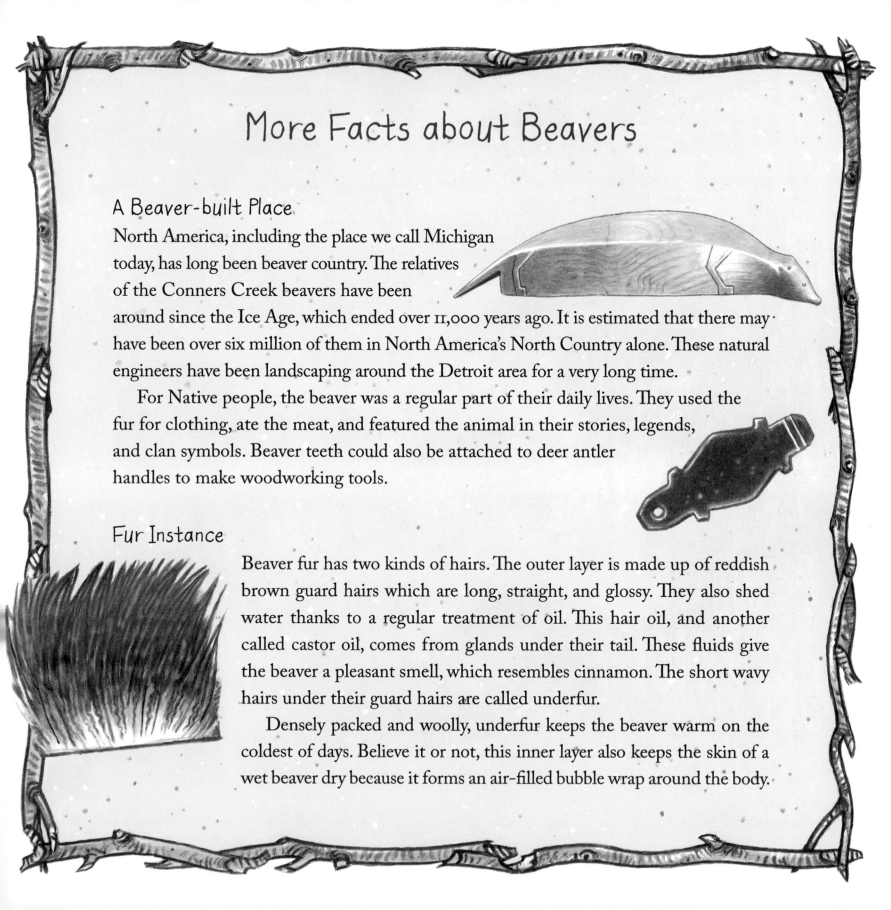

North America, including the place we call Michigan today, has long been beaver country. The relatives of the Conners Creek beavers have been around since the Ice Age, which ended over 11,000 years ago. It is estimated that there may have been over six million of them in North America's North Country alone. These natural engineers have been landscaping around the Detroit area for a very long time.

For Native people, the beaver was a regular part of their daily lives. They used the fur for clothing, ate the meat, and featured the animal in their stories, legends, and clan symbols. Beaver teeth could also be attached to deer antler handles to make woodworking tools.

Fur Instance

Beaver fur has two kinds of hairs. The outer layer is made up of reddish brown guard hairs which are long, straight, and glossy. They also shed water thanks to a regular treatment of oil. This hair oil, and another called castor oil, comes from glands under their tail. These fluids give the beaver a pleasant smell, which resembles cinnamon. The short wavy hairs under their guard hairs are called underfur.

Densely packed and woolly, underfur keeps the beaver warm on the coldest of days. Believe it or not, this inner layer also keeps the skin of a wet beaver dry because it forms an air-filled bubble wrap around the body.

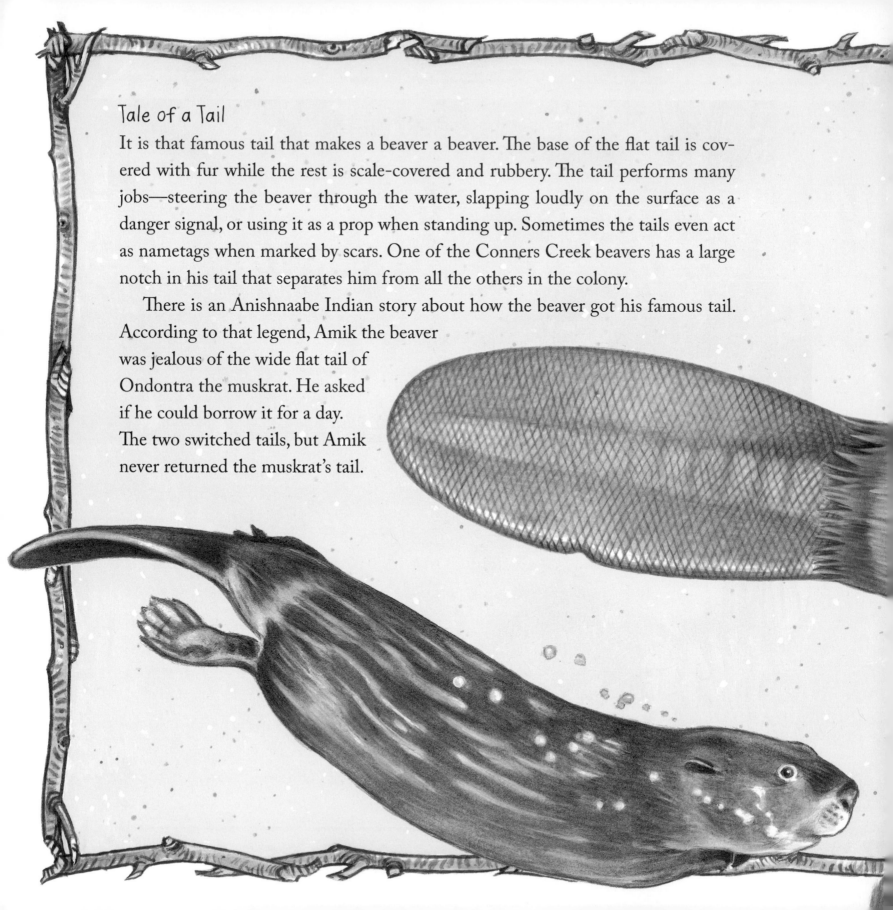

Tale of a Tail

It is that famous tail that makes a beaver a beaver. The base of the flat tail is covered with fur while the rest is scale-covered and rubbery. The tail performs many jobs—steering the beaver through the water, slapping loudly on the surface as a danger signal, or using it as a prop when standing up. Sometimes the tails even act as nametags when marked by scars. One of the Conners Creek beavers has a large notch in his tail that separates him from all the others in the colony.

There is an Anishnaabe Indian story about how the beaver got his famous tail. According to that legend, Amik the beaver was jealous of the wide flat tail of Ondontra the muskrat. He asked if he could borrow it for a day. The two switched tails, but Amik never returned the muskrat's tail.

King Castor

Beavers are members of a group of mammals called rodents, which makes them related to mice, squirrels, and muskrats. They are the largest rodents in North America and the second largest in the world (the largest is the capybara of South America). An adult beaver weighs between forty and one-hundred pounds. Like all rodents, they have four buck-toothed incisors and two rows of flat grinding teeth. Rodents are chewing animals, and the beaver takes this family trait to another level. Their king-sized orange incisors can cut through solid wood as if it were butter. Castors can even chew underwater without swallowing water because they can seal their lips behind their front teeth. They can also close their nostrils and ear openings, and cover their eyes with a clear eyelid, when swimming.

Feet are Neat

As big and bulky as they are, beavers can handle small twigs with their delicate five-toed "hands." The front feet are tucked tightly under the chin while their paddle-like hind feet are used for swimming. Beavers have a split nail on the second toe of each hind foot that they use as a comb for grooming the fur after a swim.

Good Neighbors

Many creatures, besides the muskrats and predators mentioned in this story, share the beaver's Conners Creek neighborhood. These include kingfishers, mallards, wood ducks, green heron, great blue and black-crowned night herons, map turtles, yellow perch, mayflies, and dragonflies, to name a few.

Acknowledgments

This book would not be possible without the invaluable assistance of Jason Cousino of DTE, and support from Debbie Delp, Julie Catka, and the members of the Edison Boat Club, and my very, very (did I say *very*?) patient wife Deb.

About the Author

Gerald Wykes is a retired museum and nature center director and freelance author, illustrator, and presenter. His 2014 *Michigan History Magazine* article "A Weed Goes to War" was honored as "Best Article of the Year" by the Michigan Historical Society. He also occasionally steps out from behind the computer and drawing board as the French Canadian storyteller and voyageur Alexander Boyer.

G. Wykes